SOLVING
SCIENCE
MYSTERIES

Why Do Stars Twinkle?

All About Space

Michael McMahon

PowerKiDS
press.
New York

Published in 2010 by The Rosen Publishing Group, Inc.
29 East 21st Street, New York, NY 10010

Produced and designed by Denise Ryan & Associates
Editor: Helen Moore and Edwina Hamilton
Designer: Anita Adams
Photographer: Lyz Turner-Clark
U.S. Editor: Joanne Randolph

Photo Credits: All pictures from NASA except for: p. 4 top: Image of Ted Atkins courtesy EverestMax Expedition; pp. 11, 17 top and 18 top: Photolibrary; p. 13 top: Roger Stoll; p. 19 top: AIP Emilio Segre Visual Archives, John Irwin Slide Collection; p. 22 top © www.iStockphoto.com; p. 22 bottom © www.iStockphoto.com/Yucel Yilmaz.

Library of Congress Cataloging-in-Publication Data

McMahon, Michael, 1942-
 Why do stars twinkle? : all about space / Michael McMahon.
    p. cm. — (Solving science mysteries)
 Includes index.
 ISBN 978-1-61531-895-7 (lib. bdg.) — ISBN 978-1-61531-921-3 (pbk.) —
 ISBN 978-1-61531-922-0 (6-pack)
 1. Astronomy—Miscellanea—Juvenile literature. 2. Solar system—Miscellanea—Juvenile literature. 3. Outer space—Exploration—Miscellanea—Juvenile literature. I. Title.
 QB46.M494 2010
 520—dc22
                          2009034097

Manufactured in the United States of America.

CPSIA Compliance Information: Batch #WW10PK: For Further Information contact Rosen Publishing, New York, New York at 1-800-237-9932

Contents

Questions About Space

Q: Where does space start?

A: Space begins at the outer edge of our planet's **atmosphere**. There is no sharp line that divides air and space. The atmosphere just gets thinner as you go up. On Mount Everest, which is 5.5 miles (8.8 km) high, the air is so thin that climbers have to use **oxygen** so that they can breathe. However, even at 199 miles (320 km) above sea level, there are still a few oxygen and **nitrogen molecules**. Once you are more than 621 miles (1,000 km) above sea level, though, you are beyond the last traces of the atmosphere.

Saturn surrounded
by its rings

Q: How far have people traveled in space?

A: Astronauts on Project Apollo traveled as far as the Moon, which is about 239,228 miles (385,000 km) away from Earth. Russian **cosmonaut** Valeri Poliakov traveled a distance of 174 million miles (280 million km) around Earth in the *Mir* space station.

Q: How does space travel affect people?

A: In space, people seem to become weightless. If people stay in space for a long time, the lack of **gravity** makes their muscles start to waste away. Exercise and a special diet help lessen these effects.

Q: What do astronauts do in space?

A: On space **missions**, specialists make observations and carry out experiments, such as studying the effect of spaceflight on the human body. Sometimes, they perform an extravehicular activity (EVA) when they leave the spacecraft to help rescue or repair satellites.

Questions About the Solar System

Q: How was the solar system formed?

A: The Sun and the planets, which are part of the solar system, were born in a huge cloud of cold, swirling gas and dust called the solar nebula. (You can read about nebulas on page 10.) About five billion years ago, the cloud collapsed under its own gravity into a fast-spinning, ball-shaped mass. The center part became denser and hotter and eventually became the Sun. Rocks, dust, and gases circling around the Sun then began to come together and eventually formed the planets.

Mars
diameter: 4,221 miles (6,794 km)

Venus
diameter: 7,521 miles (12,104 km)

Mercury
diameter: 3,032 miles (4,879 km)

Earth
diameter: 7,926 miles (12,756 km)

Jupiter
diameter: 88,844 miles (142,980 km)

Sun
diameter: 864,949 miles (1,392,000 km)

the Sun

Q: Are there different kinds of planets?

A: Yes, there are two kinds of planets. Jupiter, Saturn, Uranus, and Neptune are balls of gas far from the Sun. Mercury, Venus, Mars, and Earth are small, rocky planets close to the Sun. Pluto, which was called a planet until 2006, is a tiny ice world at the edge of the solar system.

Saturn
diameter: 74,900 miles (120,540 km)

Uranus
diameter: 31,764 miles (51,120 km)

Neptune
diameter: 30,777 miles (49,530 km)

Large and small

Each planet's diameter, the distance across the planet, shows that even the largest planet, Jupiter, is small when compared to the Sun.

Mercury

Venus

Q: What are the hottest planets?

A: Mercury and Venus are the hottest planets. Both planets orbit much closer to the Sun than Earth does. The innermost planet, Mercury, takes 88 days to orbit the Sun. At midday on Mercury the shade temperatures soar to 806° F (430° C) and at night they plunge to –292° F (–180° C). Venus is even hotter than Mercury. Everywhere, day and night, the temperature is a scorching 860° F (460°C).

Q: How do we know so much about Venus when it is always covered in cloud?

A: From 1989 to 1993, NASA's *Magellan* probe beamed **radar** signals at the surface of Venus. "NASA" stands for "National Aeronautics and Space Administration." The radio waves passed through the clouds, hit the surface, and bounced back to *Magellan*. This helped create a picture of Venus's surface. *Magellan* then transmitted its radio pictures to Earth.

Magellan *probe*

Q: which planet is most like Earth?

A: Mars, the "red planet," is the planet most like Earth. A day on Mars is just 40 minutes longer than our day. Mars has summer and winter seasons. Billions of years ago, Mars was almost as warm as Earth. Rivers flowed across its surface and an ocean may have covered half the land. In 1996, scientists found fossils of bacteria inside a **meteorite** from Mars. Some scientists think that this proved that there was once life on Mars.

Earth

Mars

The first Mars Exploration Rover, named *Spirit*, was launched on a Delta II rocket from Cape Canaveral, Florida. *Spirit* landed on Mars on January 4, 2004.

9

Questions About Stars, Nebulas, Galaxies, and Black Holes

The Cone Nebula is a huge cloud of gas.

Q: Why do the stars twinkle?

A: Stars, which are balls mad up mostly of hot **hydrogen**, are so far away that each of them looks like a sparkling point of light. When starlight passes through Earth's atmosphere, it travels through layers of air that bend the light backwards and forwards. This makes the stars look as if they are twinkling. If you traveled beyond Earth's atmosphere, the stars would shine steadily.

Q: What is a nebula?

A: A nebula is a huge cloud of gas and dust found in the space between the stars. Nebulas contain all the ingredients needed to form stars and planets, including atoms of hydrogen, oxygen, and nitrogen. They also contain water, **graphite**, and other molecules. Some nebulas are dark. Some nebulas glow by reflecting the light from nearby stars. Some create their own light.

The Milky Way is a spiral galaxy.

Q: What galaxy does Earth belong to?

A: Earth is part of the Milky Way galaxy. Our galaxy contains the Sun and 200 billion other stars, as well as vast clouds of gas and dust. From above, the Milky Way would look like a slowly spinning firework with spectacular spiral arms studded with young blue stars.

Q: What is a black hole?

A: A black hole is a region in space with such strong gravity that it swallows up everything that comes near it, even light. A black hole may form when a massive star blasts itself apart. The core of the star collapses so violently that all its matter is crushed into almost nothing, leaving behind an area of intense gravity—a black hole.

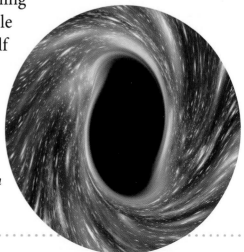

an artist's impression of a black hole

11

It's a fact

Neil Armstrong's Moon footprint

Yuri Gagarin

> The First Person in Space

Cosmonaut Yuri Gagarin was the first person in space when he made one orbit of Earth in a Vostok capsule on April 12, 1961.

> Footprint on the Moon

The footprint astronaut Neil Armstrong left on the Moon in 1969 should last for millions of years because there is no air on the Moon.

the Hubble Space Telescope

> A Space Observatory

Launched from the Space Shuttle Discovery in 1990, the Hubble Space Telescope (HST) orbits about 373 miles (600 km) above Earth. It sends back some of the most detailed images of the universe ever seen.

> What's That I Hear?

The Very Large Array (VLA) in New Mexico is one of the world's largest radio telescopes. Its 27 dish-shaped antennae can tune in to radio signals coming from planets, stars, and galaxies.

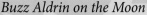
Buzz Aldrin on the Moon

> Moonwalking

There have been six Moon landings, beginning with *Apollo 11* in 1969 and ending with *Apollo 17* in 1972. During these missions 12 astronauts have explored the Moon's surface.

> Comet's Tail

As a comet orbits the Sun, its tail grows and fades but always points away from the Sun.

> A Total Eclipse of the Sun

Once every one or two years, the Moon comes directly between Earth and the Sun causing a total eclipse of the Sun. Its shadow falls in a narrow band across Earth. People who live where this shadow falls see the Moon's dark shape cover the Sun for a few minutes. All that can be seen of the Sun is the faint, outer atmosphere called the **corona**.

> Nature's Light Show

Sun storms blow particles into space. These particles sometimes come into Earth's atmosphere causing a colored glow called an **aurora**. In the northernmost or southernmost countries of the world, you can often see auroras in the night sky. They look like rippling curtains of green, red, or pink light. These amazing **phenomena** are named after the Roman goddess of the dawn, Aurora.

an aurora in the night sky

Can You Believe It?

A Great Ball of Fire

The Sun contains 99.99 percent of all the matter in the solar system. The Sun is so big that you could pack a million Earths inside it.

Dogs and Cats in Space

In 1957, a Samoyed husky called Laika was launched into space by the Russians. In 1963, the French launched a cat called Feliette into space.

Venus Spins

Venus spins backwards compared to all other planets, except Uranus. It may have been hit by an asteroid, which turned it upside down.

Mars Meltdown

If all the ice that exists on Mars melted, scientists believe that it would form an ocean between 33 feet (10 m) and 328 feet (100 m) deep.

the landscape on Mars

Venus

That's Amazing!

At the center of the Milky Way there might be a black hole that weighs as much as a million Suns.

Growing Taller

Astronauts grow 1 to 2 inches (2.5–5 cm) taller during a spaceflight. During weightlessness the **vertebrae** of their spines spread apart. When the astronauts return to Earth, they shrink back to their preflight height.

Posing in front of the orbiter Atlantis *from the left are Mission Specialists Daniel Burbank, Heidemarie Stefanyshyn-Piper and Steven MacLean; Pilot Christopher Ferguson; Commander Brent Jett; and Mission Specialist Joseph Tanner.*

Who Found out?

The Return of the comet: Edmund Halley

Edmund Halley (1656–1742) was an English astronomer and mathematician. He worked out that the apparent appearance of three separate comets through the years was actually the return of one comet every 76 years. It had been observed in Earth's skies since 240 BCE.

Halley first recorded this comet in 1682. It was named after him when he successfully predicted its return in 1758. The comet returned in 1835, 1910, and 1986. In 2062, Halley's Comet will again brighten the sky.

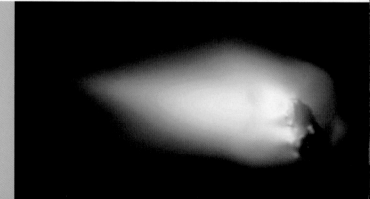

In this photograph of a comet, taken from the Giotto spacecraft, three jets can be seen blowing molecules of space matter towards the Sun.

The Discovery of Neptune: Johann Galle

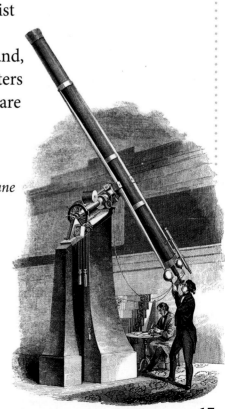

On September 23, 1846, German astronomer Johann Gottfried Galle (1812–1910) became the first person to view the planet Neptune. He used the calculations of French astronomer Urbain Le Verrier and English astronomer John Couch Adams to assist him.

Throughout his career he studied comets and, in 1894, he published a list of 414 comets. Craters on the Moon and Mars and a ring of Neptune are named in his honor.

artwork of the refractor telescope used to find Neptune

Neptune

The Milky Way:
Bartholomeus Jan Bok
and Dr. Priscilla Fairfield Bok

Dutch-American astronomer Bart Bok (1906–1983) and his American wife, Dr. Priscilla Fairfield Bok (1896–1975) mapped out the spiral arms of the Milky Way galaxy. They studied the great clouds that illuminate the constellations of Orion and Carina and tried to piece together how new stars are born from these clouds.

Dark Matter:
Dr. Vera Cooper Rubin

Dr. Vera Cooper Rubin (1928–) is an American astronomer who first drew attention to the possible existence of dark matter, calling it missing matter. Her curiosity led her to a remarkable discovery: that galaxies are surrounded by clouds of invisible dark matter. Astronomers now think that 90 percent of the matter in the universe is dark, but they still do not know what it is.

the center of the Milky Way, aglow with dust

It's **Quiz** Time!

The pages where you can find the answers are shown in the red circles, except where otherwise noted.

Can you unscramble the words so that the definitions make sense?

1. A teemriteo is a small rock or piece of metal that travels through ecasp. ㉓

2. The kliym ayw is the lagayx that contains our rolas tesyms and all the ratss you can see in the ginth sky. ⑪

3. A rast is a large ball of hydrogen sga that produces gilth and aeht. ⑩

4. A naletp is a large object, such as smar, that bortis a star such as the nsu. ⑥

Match the words in the first column to their partner in the second column.

⑥	solar	Armstrong	⑫
⑫	Space	Space Telescope	⑫
⑪	Milky	Comet	⑯
⑪	black	system	⑥
⑲	dark	eclipse of the Sun	⑬
⑯	Halley's	Gagarin	⑫
⑫	Neil	Shuttle	⑫
⑫	Yuri	hole	⑪
⑫	Hubble	Way	⑪
⑬	total	matter	⑲

Solve the space crossword.

ACROSS

1. A mixture of gases surrounding Earth, a star, or a planet (23)

4. A device used to track or locate objects which are out of sight (8)

5. A cloudy, luminous or dark patch consisting of gas and dust in the night sky (10)

7. Abbreviation for times before noon

8. The planet in the solar system seventh from the Sun (7)

11. The star around which Earth and the other seven planets of the solar system revolve (6)

DOWN

1. A glowing display in the upper layers of the atmosphere near the poles (13)

2. A colorless, odorless gas that is abundant in Earth's atmosphere (4)

3. The planet in the solar system on which we live (5)

6. The line around which a rotating body turns

7. The red planet (9)

9. Initials for the Hubble Space Telescope (12)

Answers: 7 across - AM; 6 down - axis

Try It Out!

What You'll Need:

this book, a library book on the planets or access to the Internet, paper, a stapler or three-hole punch, and some string

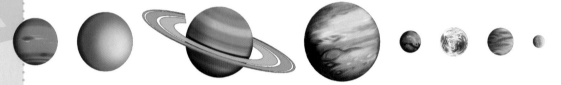

What to Do:

After reading this book, you know that our universe is a really cool place. Let's make a book about the planets.

- First do some research using this book, library books, or the Internet.
  - Then take eight sheets of paper and punch holes along one side.
- Write the name of a planet on the top of each sheet, using a separate piece for each planet.
- Draw a picture of the planet under its name on each sheet and write down a few facts about it.

Don't forget to add a cover to your book with a title and your name on it. Use the string to tie your pages together. Have fun learning about the planets!

Glossary

atmosphere (AT-muh-sfeer) The mixture of gases surrounding Earth, a star, or a planet.

aurora (uh-RAWR-uh) A glowing display in the upper layers of the atmosphere near the poles.

corona (kuh-ROH-nah) The white halo around the Sun, which is only seen during a total eclipse.

cosmonaut (KOZ-muh-naht) The Russian word for a person who goes into space.

graphite (GRA-fyt) A soft, greasy-feeling form of carbon.

gravity (GRA-vih-tee) The force existing between any two bodies because of their mass.

hydrogen (HY-dreh-jen) A colorless, odorless, inflammable gas.

meteorite (MEE-tee-uh-ryt) A small solid body from space.

missions (MIH-shunz) Assignments for a particular purpose.

molecules (MAH-lih-kyoolz) The smallest structural units into which a chemical substance can be divided and still have the properties of that substance.

nitrogen (NY-truh-jen) A colorless, odorless, chemically inactive gas.

oxygen (OK-sih-jen) A colorless, odorless gas that is abundant in Earth's atmosphere.

phenomena (fih-NO-meh-nuh) Remarkable or extraordinary objects or events.

radar (RAY-dahr) A device used to track or locate objects that are out of sight.

vertebrae (VER-tuh-bray) The chain of bones that form the backbone.

Index

Web Sites

Due to the changing nature of Internet links, PowerKids Press has developed an online list of Web sites related to the subject of this book. This site is updated regularly. Please use this link to access the list: *www.powerkidslinks.com/ssm/twinkle/*